Angel Dreams

Inspired Writings
By
Sandra J Yearman

Seraphim Publishing LLC

WE WILL BRING LIGHT TO ALL THE DARK PLACES

Registered trademark-Sandra J Yearman
Seraphim Publishing
438 Water St
Cambridge, WI 53523

Library of Congress Control Number: 2010912345
ISBN: 978-0-9841506-6-3
First Edition

Always And Forever
Is The Father's Love
Listen To The Angels Sing
The Holy Songs From Above
Amen
Amen
Amen

CONTENTS

DEDICATION

SEEKING LIGHT IN THE DARKNESS

CONTENTS

COMING HOME

Dedication

Angel Dreams

Do the Angels dream in slumber
Do they understand
Do they have the same illusions
As the world of man

Are the Angels tested
Are they sent on Holy missions
from above
Do they walk among us
As their missions of true Love

Do they whisper to us
Do we hear what they say
Or discard their voices
As an anomaly of the day

Can we really see them
Or does our mind play tricks
To keep us in the darkness
To control us in the pit

Why would God send His Angels
But to guide us through the tests
To send us His messages
To let us know that we are blessed

Amen Amen Amen

Your Holiness To Seek

God thank You for my blessings
That have sustained me on this path
of life
Thank You for the miracles
That delivered me from strife

Thank You for the Angels
The Loved Ones that You send
For guiding me on my journey
For teaching me Amen

And thank You for the journey
Without I would not see
That death can be conquered
That miracles are sent from Thee

And thank You for the Holy
opportunities
The choices, the perceptions I
would make
For it was in the journey
And the acts of Faith that I would take

That led me to Your Altar
That led me to Your feet
That picked me up when I fell
Your Holiness to seek

Amen Amen Amen

Sounds That Touch The Soul

The music in the night air
The sounds that touch the soul
The Angels dance to harmony
A sound only Heaven knows

Violins in the distance
Chimes in the trees
An Angel walks among us
As only Heaven sees

Whispers in the meadows
Doves that God sends in
Angels to gather
To bring us together again

Amen Amen Amen

God Did Send An Angel

God whispered her name upon
the earth
Her grace and love bestowed
An Angel in her elegance
Of Heaven she did know

She blessed a world of sorrow
She loved a world of pain
She moved all who met her
Of Heaven she did gain

She came when she was needed
She protected one and all
She healed by the Grace of God
She saved them from the fall

Thank You God in Heaven
For the Angels who walk among
For sending us Your Grace
For sending us Your Son

Amen Amen Amen

The Image Of The Lion

A knight he was in this realm
The world no longer knows
The courage and the honor
The sacrifice to show

Courage was his center
Faith and Love to all
The image of the Lion
Overcame the great walls

Faithful to his Master
Faithful to his Lord
The image of the Lion
The Angel with the Sword

Worlds he had traveled
Lifetimes he lived
The image of the Lion
Love and Mercy to give

Amen Amen Amen

Songs Of Long Ago

Listen to the Angels sing
Songs of long ago
Songs about our Savior
Songs that we do know

Listen to their voices
Hear them with your hearts
Listen to their love
Know we are never apart

Listen to the tenderness
Listen to the truths
Listen to the Song of God
A broken heart to soothe

Let their voices carry
With the music dance
Know that your Father Loves you
His Holy Way entrance

Amen Amen Amen

Time Of Grace

In the days of roses
In the Time of Grace
An Angel came from Heaven
To save the human race

What He found disturbed him
The tears of Heaven flow
For the plight of creation
For the children here below

Glory Alleluia
Glory in God's Right
'Help them' sang the Angel
'Save them from the night'

The children had forgotten
They had lost their way
The choices that they made
Their decisions to stray

From their Holy Father
From the Blessed Son
From the Holy Spirit
Their God, Three in One

Glory Alleluia
Glory in God's Right
'Help them' sang the Angel
'Save them from the night'

In the days of roses
In the Time of Grace
An Angel came from Heaven
To save the human race

Amen Amen Amen

Take The Father's Hand

Dreams in the illusions
Dreams within the storms
Hope reigns forever
The Path forever worn

Angels call unto us
Whispers in the night
Comfort comes from many
To save us from our fright

Winds that over take us
Winds that cleanse the land
Angels reach out to us
Take and Understand

Dreams in the illusions
Dreams within the storms
Hope reigns forever
The Path forever worn

Never do they leave us
Forever take a stand
The Angels reach out to us
Take the Father's Hand

Amen Amen Amen

The First Born Of Creation

He is before creation
The first born Son God sent
To teach us of His Love
And Forgiveness as it was meant

His Sacrifice for us
His Teachings and His Love
Were all Gifts from the Father
Signs of a Father's Love

Millions are the ages
Millions are the tears
That call out to the Father
To bring the Heavens near

He listens and He answers
Though some refuse to hear
His Voice in all creation
The Blessings and the tears

Amen Amen Amen

The Son Unto The Father

The Son unto the Father
Holiness abounds
The Face of Heaven shines
The children have been found

Glory Alleluia
As the Angels sing
Glory to the Father
Glory to the King

Mercy without measure
Love no limits known
Cherished are the children
Welcome them back Home

Glory Alleluia
As the Angels sing
Glory to the Father
Glory to the King

Eternal are the Teachings
Forever are the Words
Glory Alleluia
The Angel's voices heard

Amen Amen Amen

Thank God For You

Thank God for the day you were born
Thank God for your presence on
this earth
Thank all of Heaven
For the blessings of joy and mirth

You give my life meaning
With your actions and your ways
To be your mother
Is the blessing of my days

I will always love you
Until the end of time
Such a precious gift from Heaven
God's radiance sublime

Amen Amen Amen

Seeking Light In The Darkness

God Pray For Me

God pray for me
When I have no voice
When I have fallen
And I have no choice

Pray for me God
When I am lost
Filled with terror
Compromised beyond all cost

Pray for me God
When I am dead
My tears no more
Your words were said

Believe in the Father
Believe in the Son
To Conquer this world
Your Praises are sung

Amen Amen Amen

Pictures Of Darkness

Pictures of darkness
Symbols of disgrace
What must God think
Of what man has done in this place

He gave us a garden
And dominion of all
Did man witness to God
Or did God witness man's fall

Horror unspoken
Fear out of control
What is man's destiny
What is man's role

He gave us a garden
And dominion of all
Did man witness to God
Or did God witness man's fall

Killers among us
Monsters and more
Will the children of God
Ever learn how to soar

God make us worthy
Of the Gifts we receive
Increase our Faith
Help us to Believe

In Your Love and Your Mercy
In Your Presence above all
In Your Forgiveness
Heal man's great fall

Amen Amen Amen

Intolerance

All they saw was the vessel
They focused on the flaws
They said, "He wasn't right"
The differences were all they saw

They ostracized and criticized
Cruelty to Atone
They only saw with human eyes
The boy, he felt alone

God is in the Spirit
God is in the Soul
God makes no mistakes
The boy was of the fold

God sends us Angels
And Miracles to behold
The forms that they come in
Test our human mold

Jesus taught Compassion
He showed us with His Deeds
That God Loves His children
They were created from His Holy Seed

Yet, man in their intolerance
And man with their hate
Crucify God's children
And reject the Holy Gate

Amen Amen Amen

Questions

I am
Only happy when...
This question to answer
Or just pretend

I love
But is it real
Do I understand the meaning
Do I truly feel

I know
The questions to
The answers illusive
The memories true

I believe
The Word is true
The Father here
The Spirit who

Will save and comfort
Will heal and forgive
Will conquer the darkness
And help us to live

Amen Amen Amen

The Face Of Darkness

I have seen your face
I have heard your lies
I have seen your slaves
As they die

Your darkness grows
With horror and pain
You steal the souls
Again and again

And yet the illusions you create
Have no power in this place
For if just one soul
With Faith and Grace

Will stand before
The human race
And say
'You are not wanted in this place'

The world is blessed with Love
and Grace

Amen Amen Amen

The Elder Woman

'Bless you', for thinking of me
The elder woman said
For no one had taken the time
They treated her as if she was dead

Loneliness is bitter
Being forgotten tortures the soul
Why do we turn our faces
Why do we pay such tolls

The spirit in the vessel
The vessel frail and insecure
The darkness that tortures man
They refuse to look in the mirror

God Bless Your children
That they may see
Every form of life
Is a gift from Thee

Give us the hearts of Angels
Compassion and strength
Teach us to care for Your children
Help us to seek Your Face

Amen Amen Amen

A Friend I Had

A friend I had
An Angel in her right
But most only saw
That she was being destroyed by
the night

A light flickers in the darkness
So small and yet unseen
Hope for the spirit
Redemption for the being

The vessel worn and damaged
From years of abuse and decay
A spirit that was drowning
Needing a Better Way

A Hand reached into the darkness
And led her to the Light
It blessed her with Love and Mercy
And saved her from the night

Amen Amen Amen

The Horror Did Grow

The young mother died
The horror did grow
For the family that was left
Their way no longer to know

'Why did this happen'
'Who is to blame'
'What are the reasons'
'What in God's Name'

Songs on the night breeze
Float in the air
Another soul Home
Burdens no longer to bear

The answers may elude us
As our hearts break with pain
Call on the Father
His compassion to gain

Ask Him to carry
Ask Him to heal
Ask for the answers
On bended knees kneel

Ask Him to hold you
And never let go
Ask him to sustain you
His Promise to know

Amen Amen Amen

Love Cradles The Memories

Taps tore through the crisp air
Thunder roared in the night
They lay to rest a comrade
A victim of the fight

Tears throughout the ages
Mother's sorrow known
Children die in horror
The face of man is shown

Precious are the memories
That hold our hearts in place
Never will they die
Or will time erase

Love transcends all boundaries
Love transcends all wars
Love cradles the memories
The Love of Heaven pours

For the Mothers and the children
For the Fathers who in pain
Call out to the Heavens
Ask for God by Name

Amen Amen Amen

Images Of Me

How do I tell them
How do they know
Is the face that I reveal
Me or just a show

Reflections in the eyes of others
Illusions in the night
Can I reveal my soul
Why does this fill me with fright

They see me in so many roles
The parts I play to perfection
I long to tell my family
There is more to this reflection

They never ask me how I feel
Or do I dream in slumber
Do I have aspirations
More than to be a mother

Do I ever feel afraid
Or trapped within my day
Would I on Angel's wings
Sail to worlds away

God help me to overcome my fears
That my family cannot understand
The many images You have created
Of woman and of man

Amen Amen Amen

Seals

The seals to hell were broken
The demons took control
Of the ones whose hatred and fear
Led them to sell their very souls

The victims were numbed by horror
They could not comprehend
A world of darkened chaos
Where torture has no end

Man can make his choices
Man can make his pacts
Is it the demons without
Or the demons within that makes
man act

Are the demons the ones who broke
the seals
Or was it man on that dark day
When he had to make his first choice
Of night or of the Light of a
Better Way

God cleanse us of our darkness
Please take control of each
and every life
Help us to find You
Redeem us from our strife

Forgive us for our hatred
Help us to take responsibility
Is it the demons without
Or the demons within that we
really see

Amen Amen Amen

Believe Unto The Lord

A few stood against the many
On a battlefield of old
As a voice cried into the abyss
As a Light showed the Way Home

Bravery exists in many vessels
The kind and size unknown
Until they face the battle
The choice to follow the path Home

On this day of ages
The battle songs do ring
Who do you bow to
The world or to your King

Darkness asks for submission
A choice for to regret
The Love of Heaven awaits
Those who can resist the darkest test

A child can stand before giants
A man before the hoard
Faith is the strongest weapon
Believe unto the Lord

Amen Amen Amen

The Madness

We sleep to escape the madness
Then our nightmares turn to pain
And we are brought back into
the darkness
Of Man's realities again

Illusions within illusions
Man's realities
Beleaguered in the dreams
Consumed with maladies

Angels speak through the nightmares
Follow the sweetness of their sound
Pray that they will hold you
And take you Heaven bound

Amen Amen Amen

Loss So Unexpected

Loss unexpected
Hearts filled with pain
Questions asked of God
Again and Again

Life, it is so fragile
With its pain and with its grace
Spirits soar to Heaven
And surpass all time and space

Some say life is a tapestry
Or a journey we must take
To grow and to conquer darkness
To learn from our mistakes

The pain of losing loved ones
The mystery of it all
The absence without solace
The void within the wall

Know that God is with us
He cradles and He holds
He understands life's mysteries
He blesses all our souls

Layers of illusions
Only God knows what is real
Have Faith that He will prevail
And our hearts He will heal

Amen Amen Amen

The Pipes Play

The pipes play in the distance
Another comrade lost
Wars throughout the ages
Do we win what we have sought

The brave and the human
Conquer demons within and without
To walk through a nightmare
They may never get out

We do not remember
We cannot forget
The loss and the sacrifice
The darkness of the pit

God send them a light in the darkness
A star to show them the way
So they know that You are with them
And will turn darkness into day

Let the Angels pray for them
And save them in the night
Let the Holiness of Heaven
Stand before them in their plight

Amen Amen Amen

Coming Home

Dreams

The voices that whisper
Heard upon the wind
Speaking to children
To let God in

The voices we remember
The voices we recognize
The voices we deny
The voices we disguise

Do only children
Hear the Angel's voices
Are the voices denied
By the adult choices

Heard in our dreams
The melody of old
The Song of the Angels
Before souls were sold

In our dreams
Do we remember when
We knew our Home
Which has no end

Amen Amen Amen

I Will Fight Your Dragons

I will fight your dragons
I will carry you on Wings of Gold
I will stand before you
The Holy Songs of old

I will slay the monsters
That terrorize the night
I will show you Mercy
I will send My Light

I will send you the Jewel of Heaven
The Glory and the Son
The Promise of the Father
The Holy Three in One

Amen Amen Amen

The Desert

I walked in the desert
I thought I was alone
In truth, I took a journey
And found my way back Home

The days turned into darkness
The nights they were so long
I stumbled and I fell
I had forgotten the Song

The desert it called to me
The voices of the night
My body filled with pain
My soul was filled with fright

I walked in the desert
I thought I was alone
In truth, I took a journey
And found my way back Home

The shadows overtook me
They sought to take control
The choices that I made
I almost lost my soul

When the shadows were the darkest
When the night, it was so long
An Angel spoke to me
And helped me to remember the Song

We sang that Song together
As God's Light shown in
The shadows fell before us
The terror and the sin

I walked in the desert
I thought I was alone
In truth, I took a journey
And found my way back Home

Amen Amen Amen

The Tiger In The Storm

I will search the darkest night
I will roam within the storm
I will seek out the lost
The tarnished and the worn

I will spread my wings to cover
I will sing to you of God
I will protect you from the night
I will go were ever you have trod

And in the midst of chaos
The horror and the fear
Pray to the Heavens
And know the Angels are near

I will send you a golden cord
To clutch to in your fright
I will never let go
To lose you in the night

I will talk; but will you listen
Will you turn my Love away
Will you accept the Grace of God
Or in the storm to stay

And in the midst of chaos
The horror and the fear
Pray to the Heavens
And know the Angels are near

Amen Amen Amen

Our Spirits Entwine

I whispered in his ear
Wait for me I said
To my friend who was dying
After such a life we had led

I cannot follow you now
On your journey Home
My heart is filled with sorrow
My life seems all alone

The memories we created
Will always be a part
Of the song my soul sings
A place within my heart

Never in my wildest dreams
Did I think God would bless
Me with such a friend
So far above the rest

And when again we meet
In our Heavenly Home
Our spirits to entwine
Our souls no more to roam

Amen Amen Amen

Always

Always and forever
My Presence to you is near
Call out to the Heavens
Ask My Voice to hear

Always and forever
Are the Promises I make
Listen for My guidance
Listen for Life's sake

Always and forever
Eternity be told
Pray to the Father, Son and Spirit
Heaven to behold

Always and forever
Is the Father's Love
Listen to the Angels sing
The Holy Songs from above

Amen Amen Amen

Holy Flame

I Love you now
As I Loved your fathers
I AM your God
There is no other

My Son, the Spirit
We are Three in One
The Heavenly Song
Forever is sung

I have been with you forever
And forever will reign
Call upon Me
All Holiness to gain

I have sent many teachers
The Messiah of all
Do not cast Me out
Do not perpetuate the great fall

Talk to me forever
Call out my Name
I will send you guides
Follow the Holy Flame

Amen Amen Amen

Abby's Song

We have been friends
So long, my dear
I still remember the day
That you finally smiled and drove
your demons away

Trust is never given
For the victims of the night
My friend, the beginning of your life
Was consumed with terror and fright

A friend that you referred to
You called her a brilliant star
Guided you from the darkness
You traveled, oh so far

And your journey led you
To love beyond compare
The home you always wanted
Safe, you could feel there

Years, I often wondered
About that friend you speak of
If she really existed
Or was the hope of one deprived
of love

Then one day I saw her
An Angel in her right
A light so brilliant
As to dissolve the darkest night

And all the years that followed
You spoke of her with love
The friend that saved you
The gift sent from above

And now that you are dying
You say you are not alone
Your brilliant friend has returned
And she will take you Home

Amen Amen Amen

Why Would God Send His Angels
But To Guide Us Through The Tests
To Send Us His Messages
To Let Us Know That We Are Blessed
Amen
Amen
Amen

9 780984 150663